12 Concepts for World Service Workbook

By George B

Introduction

1. What are the Twelve Concepts for World Service?

2. What do they detail?

3. What is the "aim" of the Twelve Concepts?

4. Why may alterations need to be made?

5. What may these Concepts provide to future generations?

6. What do the following mean?
    a. *"Right of Decision"*

    b. *"Right of Participation"*

    c. *"Right of Appeal"*

    d. *"Right of Petition"*

7. What else do the Concepts carefully delineate?

8. What should future advocates of structural change do?

9. What can easily be amended in most cases?

10. What should each amendment be appropriately labeled?

11.Why should the original Concepts be kept intact for future reference?

12. Why was the democratic set-up selected?

13. What idea pervade the Concepts?

14. What is each Concept?

15. What is each Concept a summation of?

16. What are the Twelve Concepts for World service to be added to?

Concept I

"Final responsibility and ultimate authority for A.A. world services should always reside in the collective conscience of our whole fellowship."

1. Who holds the ultimate responsibility and final authority for world services?

2. Why did authority have to be transferred to the entire fellowship?

3. What was the first step?

4. What was this body called?

5. What was the trusteeship designed for?

6. How much did the membership of A.A. increase in the ten years following the establishment of the Foundation?

7. What had been written and adopted?

8. Why were the world services so vital to A.A.?

9. Why did some people between 1945 to 1950 think that nothing could happen to A.A., that the future was guaranteed?

10. What does the average member think, even today, about A.A. World Services?

11. What had been opposed by the Trustees?

12. What was the "clincher"?

13. What shook the confidence of A.A.in 1948?

14. What were Bill and Dr. Bob concerning the Trustees?

15. What was the fact about A.A.s Founders that had to be faced?

16. What was seen as the only creditable replacement for Bill and Dr. Bob?

17. What did Bill and Dr. Bob do?

18. Why are people still vague about "group conscience"?

19. What do we know about extensive disobedience to the principles of A.A.?

20. What destiny for A.A. that we trust in God in his wisdom for, do we look forward to?

Concept II

"The General Service Conference of A.A. has become, for nearly every practical purpose, the active voice and effective conscience of our whole Society in our world affairs."

1. Why can't A.A. Groups and A.A. members do for the worldwide membership?

2. What is the power of the groups and members?

3. What must the groups and members do to accomplish the services needed?

4. What did Dr. Bob and Bill hold in 1937?

5. Who did they have to find to help them?

6. What was the process of delegation they established?

7. What did the Board of Trustees eventually control completely?

8. What area came next?

9. What kind of "charge" did the Board of Trustees eventually control?

10. What difference became apparent?

11. Where did the ultimate authority for world services ultimately become vested?

12. What group was given ultimate authority?

Concept III

"To insure effective leadership, we should endow each element of A.A. – the Conference, the General Service Board and its service corporations, staffs, committees, and executives – with a traditional "Right of Decision."

1. What is the "Right of Decision"?

2. Under what concept are the ultimate authority and final responsibility for world services held?

3. The Conference and General Service Board Charters define what?

4. What does good management seldom mean?

5. Why does a traditional and practical principle have to be used to continually balance the right relations between ultimate authority and delegated responsibility?

6. The solution to this problem is to be found where?

7. What will there be to correct inefficiency, ineffectiveness, or abuse?

8. How should the *"Right of Decision"* be practically applied?

   A.

   B.

   C.

9. The *"Right of Decision"* should never be made an excuse for what?

10. Our entire A.A. Program rests squarely upon what?

Concept IV

"At all responsible levels, we ought to maintain a traditional "Right of Participation," allowing a voting representation in reasonable proportion to the responsibility that each must discharge."

1. What does the Charter specifically provide?

2. What is the make-up of the Directors of A.A. World Services?

3. Who is traditionally the general manager?

4. Each director has what kind of vote?

5. What is the mission of the Trustees?

6. What does the corporate or participating management style permit?

7. How are the Grapevine directors elected?

8. What is there none of when it comes time to vote?

9. What is the one exception to the membership of the Board of Trustees?

10. Who do the Trustees traditionally invite to the Board meetings?

11. Why did the early Trustees think they had a duty to manage everything themselves?

12. What happens every time an absolute authority is established

13. What did the Founders finally see about authority?

14. No one is against the idea of what kind of authority?

15. Whose votes should we always allow? Why?

16. What is the shining ideal of the A.A. organization?

17. What kind of function is the "Right of Participation"?

18. What does our participation assure us?

Concept V

"Throughout our structure, a traditional "Right of Appeal" ought to prevail, so that minority opinion will be heard and personal grievances receive careful consideration."

1. Who should be encouraged to file minority reports? When?

2. What do minority appeals generate?

3. What does this option refrain existing authority from doing?

4. The well-heard minority protects us from what?

5. Any member of our service structure can petition for what?

6. The *Rights of "Appeal"* and *"Petition"* aim at what?

7. When is an alcoholic a member of A.A.?

8. What can we not force a member to do?

9. Who can act for a Group Conscience when it cannot act for itself?

10. What democratic principle may occasionally be denied?

11. To increase deference to minority opinion better than?

12. What is evidence of real prudence and courteous deference to minority views?

13. What has been granted to all minorities?

14. What kind of government do we need to maintain?

15. What kind of tyranny will we never be subject to?

Concept VI

"The Conference recognizes that the chief initiative and active responsibility in most world service matters should be exercised by the trustee members of the Conference acting as the General Service Board."

1. What must the Conference delegate?

2. What does A.A.'s Board of Trustees critically need?

3. What is our service Charter cable to have done to it?

4. Why is the Board of Trustees given such wide latitude?

5. Why is the Board of Trustees given such wide latitude?

6. What is always our objective? Why does it need an effective business operation?

7. Why was a corporate form of business selected?

8. Why must the Trustees be given such large powers?

Concept VII

"The Charter and Bylaws of the General Service Board are legal instruments, empowering the trustees to manage and conduct world service affairs. The Conference Charter is not a legal document; it relies upon tradition and the A.A. purse for final effectiveness."

1. What is contradictory about this Concept?

2. What does this Concept mean in terms of power?

3. What kind of interest do the Trustees NOT have in the General Service Conference?

4. What position did the Trustees need to be put into?

5. Who makes new Trustee choices?

6. What balance in maintained between the Trustees and the Conference?

7. What rights should both the Trustees and the Conference avoid?

8. What absolute right do the Trustees have?

9. What are the three examples of necessary veto by the Trustees?
   A.

   B.

   C.

10. What won't either entity be tempted to make out of the other?

Concept VIII

"The trustees are the principal planners and administrators of overall policy and finance. They have custodial oversight of the separately incorporated and constantly active services. Exercising this through their ability to elect all the directors of these entities."

1. What are the heavy obligations of the Board of Trustees?

2. What is the board expected to do?

3. What must the Board do in many lesser matters?

4. What kind of oversight does the Board exercise?

5. What kind of situations does the Board mediate?

6. In effect, what is the General Service Board?

7. What has produced a more effective and harmonious business environment?

8. Why can't the General Service Board be made into an operating corporation?

9. Combining everything into one corporation would create what problems?

10. What is there always a powerful connection between?

11. What are we urged to avoid in the future?

12. What can't we convert the General Service Board into?

Concept IX

"Good service leadership at all levels is indispensable for our future functioning and safety. Primary world leadership, once exercised by the founders, must necessarily be assumed by the trustees."

1. What shall we have a continuous problem with?

2. What couldn't A.A. function without?

3. Who should Groups take care electing? Why?

4. What has to be cast aside during these elections?

5. What should be the most important thought for elections?

6. What is the principal theme of this Concept?

7. How did the Board of Trustees operate in the first years of A.A.?

8. Why did the Board need a permanent linkage to A.A.?

9. Was making the Trustees directly accountable to A.A. a good idea? Why?

10. What is a critical turning point in a new organization?

LEADERSHIP IN A.A.

1. No society can function without what?

2. What "poles' does A.A. leadership need to function between?

3. What is the statement from A.A. literature about leaders?

4. Who is a leader in A.A.?

5. What does good leadership generate?

6. What does a group leader do?

7. What is a "politico"?

8. What is a "statesman"?

9. What will a good leader never do?

10. What is fatal for leadership?

11. What should a good leader always try to exercise?

12. What is the ability to compromise cheerfully called?

13. What should we always carefully listen to?

14. What ability is "vision"?

15. What is vision the essence of?

16. What were all the Traditions of A.A. at first?

17. What vital activity must we be proficient at?

18. What attributes will we be in continual need of?

19. What basis should we select leadership on?

20. Every sponsor is necessarily what?

Concept X

"Every service activity should be matched by an equal service authority, with the scope of the authority well defined."

1. What sound principles do most societies and governments deviate from?

2. What principle has been maintained throughout the discussions of the structure of A.A. organization?

3. What is the outstanding characteristic of every good organizational structure?

4. What is the first characteristic of any working structure?

5. What principle runs clear through our structure?

6. When delegated authority is working well, what should not happen? Why?

7. How has each level of authority been accomplished?

    a.

    b.

    c.

8. What is used to prevent delegates from over-directing the Directors?

9. What has been emphasized about the General Service Board being changed into?

10. How are conflicts avoided?

11. In all matters of joint or conflicting authority, what must be established?

12. What should always be made clear?

13. What are the two other methods that are used to make delegated authority equal to delegated responsibility?

14. Group conscience is what?

15. Who has delegated authority?

Concept XI

"The trustees should always have the best possible committees, corporate service directors, executives, staff, and consultants. Composition, qualifications, induction procedures, and rights and duties will always be matters of concern."

1. Who will the longtime success of the General Service Board depend upon?

2. Who forms the visible image of A.A.'s General Service Board?

3. What are the standing committees of the General Service Board?

   a.

   b.

   c.

4. What are the active service boards?

   a.

   b.

5. What is the General Service Board not suitable for?

6. What problems are common to both General Services Inc. and the A.A. Grapevine?

   a. Status of executives – executive direction and policy formation.

   b. Paid workers – how compensated.

   c. Rotation among staff workers.

d. Full "Participation" of paid workers is highly important

Concept XII

"The Conference shall observe the spirit of A.A. tradition, taking care that it never becomes a sea of perilous wealth of power; that sufficient operating funds and reserve be its prudent financial principle; that it place none of its members in a position of unqualified authority over others; that it reach all important decisions by discussion, vote, and, whenever possible, by substantial unanimity; that its actions never be personally punitive nor incitement to public controversy; that it never performs and act of government, and that, like the Society it serves, it will always maintain democratic in thought and action."

1. What does Concept 12 consist of?

2. What is the Conference Charter when taken as a whole?

3. What do all the Warrantees have for A.A.?

4. What do the Warrantees of Article 12 consist of?

5. What do these Warrantees indicate?

6. They are the sum of our protection against what?

7. What is the Conference named in regards to the Traditions?

8. What are the Warrantees of Article 12?

    a. Warranty One:

    b. Warranty Two:

    c. Warranty Three:

d. Warranty Four:

e. Warranty Five:

f. Warranty Six:

9. What do we A.A.'s possess more than any other fellowship in the world?

10. What do we expect that our Conference will try to act in a spirit of what?

11. The sum of these several attitudes and practices is the very essence of what in action and spirit?

12. What will ever be the quest of Alcoholics Anonymous?